36 Months

3 Years of Healing
Through Social Media Posts

Book 1

Lisa J. Smith

Peeps Publishing

PP

36 Months
3 Years of Healing Through Social Media Posts
Book 1
By Lisa J. Smith

Copyright © 2012
Published and distributed by Peeps Publishing

The author of this book does not dispense medical or mental health information. The author is merely stating her opinions and thoughts and it is not to be used as a substitute for any medical, emotional, psychological, or physical care. The intent of the author is to offer information of a general nature to uplift and inspire. It does not substitute for any health care for any person. If you choose to use any of this book for your own personal well being, it is at your own free will and risk and the author is not, and will not, be held responsible.

ISBN-13: 978-0985144807
ISBN-10: 0985144807

Peeps Publishing
PP

Dedication

This book is dedicated to everyone who believed in me, even when I did not believe in myself. Thank you for being the wind beneath my wings. Together, we can change the world.

Acknowledgments

There are so many people I want to thank. I would not be the person I am without every person I have met. Whether for a moment, a period of time in my life, or for a lifetime, many of these thoughts have been inspired by you.

First my Allie, from the time you were born I knew you arrived to teach people to raise the bar for themselves. I am no exception. I believe you started with your parents and continue to this day by inspiring others to be the best they can be. You're beautiful and gentle, yet strong being, has taught me more than you will ever know. You saved my life when you were born. You continue to show your strength, voice and soulful beauty to all that you meet today. You have been witness to my darkest days over the past 36 months. You showed up again, 22 years later, for me to rise above the hardest of times. I only hope that I have been able to be there for you in the way that you have been there for me. I love you and I cannot believe that I actually get to be your mom. You always have been a blessing to all that you meet. You are a light in the dark that shines brighter everyday.

My Andrew, from the time you were born you have challenged all that you met, starting with me. Your unique way of being in the world showed me that no two people are alike and we must learn to adapt to what we are given. God has blessed you with an amazing gift called Autism. That gift makes your life very difficult at times. The past 18 years have been nothing less than miraculous, trying, heart wrenching and beautiful. You have shown me what true and soulful bravery, strength, compassion, acceptance, perseverance and tolerance truly are. Thank you for being my teacher. They say learning is never easy and that is very true. You are a master teacher and I am blessed that you thought so much of my strength that you would pick me to be your mom. I adore every breath you take. You are my baby and I love you.

To Smitty, I would not be nearly the person I am today without you. The two decades I have spent with you have taught me so much. You have been the wind beneath my wings and the storm that sunk the ship. You truly have been one of my greatest teachers and I will always be eternally grateful for you. My journey with you helped me to find my truth, spread my wings and not be afraid to believe in myself. You taught me to trust and feel safe within my intuition so that I could help other people with theirs. I will pay it forward, carry on and know that nothing is ever what we think. Thank you Smitty for being more than I ever thought a person could be. I had to go back to the beginning. Thank you for being part of my history.

To Mom, Dad, Mark, Joey, Grandmas Jane and my late Grandma Jessie, thank you! It's true that blood runs thicker than water. You have each given me much to much and I am grateful for the blood the binds. It's funny how spirituality finds us regardless of being taught or not. The Kod's rock! I am proud to call you my family.

To my friends who broke my heart and for those who held my heart together. I would not be the person that I am today without EACH one of you! I love you more than you will ever know…all of you.

Steve, what can I say? You found me at the most broken time of my life and allowed me a place to laugh, heal and learn to love. You are my "best girlfriend ever". There is not a moment that goes by that I do not thank God for you in my life. Thank you for being born, thank you for all that you have given and that you continue to do for me today. I look forward to a lifetime of laughter, joy and love with you. You hold the space, you let me be me and accept me for who I am. You have taught me that who I am, and have always been, is beautiful and perfect and that there is, "nothing wrong with me". Finally, your editing was priceless. What a metaphor for life, huh?

For my 'Peeps', thank you for being my sanity, insanity, voices in my head, guidance, teachers, believers, healers and warriors. Your teachings have taught me that nothing is ever what we think it is. I appreciate you for being my eyes when I could not see, the voices when I could not speak and the life force that runs through my being in every moment. I am alive. I am forever grateful for all that is. I know I have 'fired and re-hired" you many times. I may not be the easiest assignment on earth but I love you more than anything and I know you love me too.

Francie, what would I do without the best editor in the world. Not only are you excellent at what you do, you are speedy as well. Thank you for being my other set of eyes when I could not see anymore. I am grateful for all that you do for me today and everyday. I love you.

And finally, to my listeners, clients and all those who said, "you need to write a book". There will never be enough words to thank you for all you gave and continue to give. This book would NEVER have been possible without your constant belief, loving nagging, pushing, strength, and intuition. You are my inspiration, my warriors and my rock stars. Little did I know I have been writing this book along. I will always be grateful to you for believing in me until I could believe in myself.

Lisa J.

From the Serenity Prayer

God grant me the serenity
to accept the things I cannot change;
courage to change the things I can;
and wisdom to know the difference.

-Reinhold Niebuhr

Introduction

These are not just random thoughts. Each page captures a moment in time that reflects where I, as well as many other people, have found themselves through different times in their life. Not unlike a photograph that captures a place in time, these words capture that time in mine as well.

Words are a beautiful thing. Letters, which are no more than individual symbols, when put together in various ways, bring life to thoughts. Words; they bring action to causes, feelings to tears, laughter to joy, understanding to misunderstanding and peace to war. Letters and words are a highly underestimated and a misunderstood tool that we as humans have taken for granted. Social media access has given us an outlet to put our thoughts into words so we can now share our inner most feelings with the world. Social media takes words to a whole new level. Healing has now become universal.

Although it's true that actions speak louder than words, without words, how would we communicate and share?

Helen Keller said, "The best and most beautiful things in the world cannot be seen or even touched - they must be felt with the heart".

Words at times cannot be seen or heard, they can only be felt. It's the feeling of the words that we feel so deeply. It's within the community of our social media platforms that we are able to bring our thoughts to form words.

36 Months of random thoughts was written during a difficult and dark, yet cathartic period of my life. Most pages are happy and positive thoughts. A few were written out of frustration and all were written out of love. I hope for each person they are inspirational, thought provoking, full of wisdom and guidance. I wanted to share what I was feeling with the hopes of connecting with other people who may be feeling the same way. There is healing in numbers.

Whether you are going through a dark time in your life, looking for inspiration or looking for a tool that can inspire and uplift you, 36 Months can help you to see that no thought is ever created by just one person. If I have the thought, then you have had the thought. So why write a book about thoughts? Why write a book about what you already are thinking? All of this has been said many times before in different ways. How much is ever really new? It's important because detaching from ourselves, seeing ourselves from a different perspective and hearing things in a different way, helps bring clarity and purpose to our lives. I have always said, "change your perception and change your life".

Isn't it interesting that today, with unlimited access to social media platforms, our journals and innermost thoughts are publicly displayed? It's similar to willingly standing in front of the mirror, naked, for the world to see. Anyone we choose can view our thoughts, dreams, frustrations, anger, hearts and minds. We don't think twice about what we share. Everything is in the moment, permanent and real. The deepest most inner thoughts we have we now share with strangers around the world. Our posts are then left defenseless against peering eyes to be interpreted according to others paradigms, experiences and journeys.

The World Wide Web is literally a web. An intangible weave, where we can say, be and connect with others around the world. Some people challenge our every thought, posting and status update. Others share with their friends and then thank you for your latest pondering. Others say nothing at all. Twenty years ago sharing our deepest thoughts, publicly, for the world to see was unthinkable. Today it is expected.

So why post on social media sites? Why share? Sometimes we write for ourselves. Sometimes we write for others. Sometimes we write for social causes and others for pop culture. For whatever the reason, many people in today's ever shrinking world feel the need to write what they are thinking. After re-reading my posts, dozens of times while writing this book, I believe we write because it makes us feel better. It gives us a sense of purpose knowing that these wonderful little words can possibly inspire another.

Our thoughts and ponderings have the ability to give people around the world the motivation they need to get through another workday. Our thoughts can lend comfort when our friends grieve. Our thoughts can make people smile. They can help others see how far they have come. Finally, we can empower others to acknowledge their own thoughts and feelings as we inspire them to overcome.

Reflecting back on this book, it is now obvious to me that most of my social media posts were written, not just for others, but for me as well. At the time, I was sure they were written for you with truths that I could relate to. It's a beautiful irony when we heal. We are actually healing ourselves.

I decided to collect some of my ponderings from my social media pages and put them together in a collection of random and heartfelt offerings. I have already shared these with many friends around the world. Now they are being shared outside of social media.

Who am I to write a book about such things? Why is that what I have to say important? It is not. It's not any more important than what you have to say. I know what I know because besides being a mom, a good friend, a bad friend, a daughter, a granddaughter, a sister, an ex-wife and whatever other roles I find myself in…I am an intuitive.

I am what some call a psychic. Others call me a medium. Some just call me a fraud and fake. Depends who you ask, their paradigms and the day you ask it. At the end of the day, what I am is a person who stands between two worlds. I am sensitive to energy. As I say, 'I know things'. If you think one world is tough to be in, try standing balanced between two. I don't say that to complain. I feel very blessed everyday to do the work I do. I have been privileged to help thousands of people find closure, change their perspective and heal. Most of the thoughts, ponderings and meanderings move through me. I am more often than not more surprised than anyone to read what I have written. Looking back, I see they were written for me more than anyone else.

For many years I hosted and produced a three hour daily talk show for CBS radio. The show was centered around using my intuition. Before listeners called in, they were looking for me to tell them their future and wanted to connect with their loved ones on the other side. After they called, they did not only leave with answers, they left with tools, laughter, tears and most of all a sense of belonging to a community of like minded people. The messages that same through were always wise and full of love. We learned together. We inspired each other. We learned to rise above the ashes holding hands and laughing all while we shed some tears together.

Many of the people I work with daily also have inspired these thoughts. Where else do they come from but from our journey. You are all a part of that for me. A journey that is full of teachers, mazes of self-discovery, wonder, confusion and most of all, love.

As much as people may believe that I have all the answers, I simply do not. I am learning and growing everyday and doing my best to stay in the moment. I have faith in every moment, and I have to believe all is as it should be. Sometimes that is easier said than done.

My vision statement, as you will read in the book, is to "Empower people to see, hear, feel, sense and know what they already do know…not what they don't". I am not here to be your next best psychic. I am not here to convince you that your loved ones are always with you by giving you messages that you want to hear. I do not tell people what they want, but I do tell them what they need. I do not judge I just pass on the messages to you. I am not here to prove anything to you other than no one ever dies and we are always connected. You are loved and you have all the tools you need. We will always be ok and love always does win out.

Throughout this book, you may hear me refer to my guides, the angels, my peeps, energy, loved ones, etc. Many of my clients and listeners have heard me use these terms before. They are terms that I use to explain what's happening in the world around me at that moment. You may call it heaven, you may call it the other side or you may call it nothing at all. At the end of the day, it simply just is whatever it is. We may never know.

This book is not about being psychic, connecting with your loved ones, energy work, or any new age or metaphysical science. It's not a book about my being a psychic, a medium, intuitive medium or whatever else you may call it. That is what I do, it is not who I am. I am just like you. This book is meant to inspire new ways of thinking and empower you to look at your situations and relationships differently than you did before.

In addition, it is to show you that each one of us have 'our days'. Good days, bad days and all days in between. Many of the self-help and new age books tell you ways to become whole. I would like you to realize that you already are. Many books give you techniques and tools to be free from your negative thinking, your egos and your mind.

They encourage you to change that in which you are, to become happier, live lighter and be better. I want to give you tools to accept who you are right now. Living and life is about the journey. The journey is who you are today. This book is for you to live in YOUR truth, accept life as it is right now, begin to look at things differently and rise above what is not working.

Please note, at the end of this book you will find a section for you to write. Copy your posts or create new ones. Express yourself the way you feel guided in the moment. This is a place for you to simply just be.

At the end of the day we are all the same. We connect by releasing and sharing our thoughts. It's easy to sit behind a little machine that hides you from the world. It's easy to hide behind a screen where the only thing people see, is what you want them to see. Posting on social media takes what's inside, our truths, and shares them with the outside world. It is scary to put my inner most ponderings, frustrations and thoughts out there for the world to read. Although, looking back I realize I have done that already and how truly healing it was. Now, I am putting them out there again. The healing never ends.

Until next time…I wish you nothing but love, light and peace in all of your moments.

Enjoy!

Lisa J. Smith

36 Months

3 Years of Healing Through Social Media Posts

Book 1

A grasshopper can only play music with its legs when it's not moving.

♥LjS

Why is self-love so hard?
In the end, the only person we leave with is our self.
We come in with us…and somewhere in between we lose
'us'. Interesting how the journey works!

♥LjS

I have decided I know nothing.

♥ LjS

Synchronicity

Anything can happen, in anyway, at anytime.

The world is a magical place filled with beautiful alignments just waiting for us...

All we have to do is get out of our own way, stay in the 'action of flow' and ALLOW the world to do its thing. The rest is magic!

Today:

Just show up for your life and do your thing...the rest is being conspired for you!

You are loved!

Xoxox

♥LjS

Sometimes the lives of others and how they chose to live puts perspective on your life and can help put some things in place...

I believe and sometimes forget that.

MOST everything we concern ourselves with, really doesn't matter...and what matters most, we least concern ourselves with. Life is over once you blink...100% true.

Please do your best to concern yourself with what really matters...if you don't know what that is...feel your heart.

Do not think with your mind.

Life may seem to drag on forever at times...but truly it is a blip...be happy and smile...be kind and be beautiful...smile and know you are love...
Live and love with all your heart while you can...
it really is a gift.

♥LjS

Sometimes the only thing left is the 3-finger salute. In
computer terms that means delete.
Don't say I didn't warn ya.

♥LjS

Message of the Moment:

Let the bad fish go...
They just end up smelling up the entire basket!

♥ LjS

Message of the Moment:

Whatever you are unhappy about right now,
it will not stay this way...
It is all only a moment and it will pass...
You are being thought about right now.

♥LjS

To be impatient shows the universe lack and
what you don't have, gratitude shows what you do have.

♥LjS

Message of the Moment:

Why does it take so long to do what we were born to do?

♥LjS

Thank you MLK for teaching ALL people to dream and to
have strength, courage and perseverance.
You have, and will always be, MY hero!!!
I KNOW you would be so proud of how far we have come.
We still have so far to go.
I hope I always make YOU proud.

♥LjS

There is no need for greatness...

The desire 'to be great' diminishes the journey of being.

As the state of being diminishes...therefore does the joy.

Being great brings joy...

To desire greatness brings anything but.

♥LjS

Change...change everything

As they say, go big or stay home!

♥LjS

Being grateful for what you do have...

aspiring and reaching for your hearts truth...

brings freedom from lack.

♥LjS

Be the grasshopper.

Knowing when and how far to leap is the key.

One must wait patiently in the grass, intuitively knowing when and how far to leap.

While waiting to leap…play in the moment.

♥LjS

Nothing is what you think it is

♥LjS

The funny thing about people who drink the Kool-Aid....

I think they are so buzzed from the sugar they don't think straight.

Maybe smell the flowers instead.

♥LjS

Ohhh the things we learn

About life…

About living…

About people…

♥LjS

Being aware of the moment is the key to movement...

Ironic huh?

♥LjS

To teach what we have learned is to

share life...give love...and rise above the limitations

we place on ourselves.

♥LjS

You can be good at what you do

but if you, yourself, don't know that...

well it's kind of like swimming into the ocean

and trying to get across without a life preserver.

♥LjS

I've learned that wanting other people to believe in our dreams is because we don't have the courage to believe in them ourselves...

♥LjS

Message of the Moment:

If we're all are writing different stories, can we ever really be on the same page?

♥ LjS

If we learn anything from the movie award shows...

It's not just trusting what you know works…it's trusting and chancing what they say won't.

♥LjS

If you forget where you come from...

Where else are you going to go?

♥LjS

If we knew we were APPROVED....
we wouldn't need to ask.

♥LjS

It's 72 degrees in my inside world.
17 degrees in the outside world.

Shorts, no shoes, t-shirts, light, green plants...
a beautiful day in Casa da Lisa.

I am SO grateful for a roof over my head, four walls and
warmth.

Thank you universe...
Today all my needs are met and it will be a great day.

♥LjS

How blessed I AM

♥LjS

A diamond in the rough...
This has always been near and dear to my heart.

Those few words bring all I need.

♥LjS

My office...

The best place to be on cold snowy days.

It's warm, cozy and full of light.

♥LjS

Feeling so blessed by spirit right now...

Connecting with my old listeners and giving messages from spirit...

NOTHING BETTER!

How can one girl be so lucky?

I must have done SOMETHING right...a BIG THANK YOU to you for being my ROCK STARS!

When you receive messages, I receive messages.

I feel so blessed as well.

Here is to turning corners and making things happen...

♥LjS

There is a lid for every pot.
This brings me great comfort.

♥LjS

Feel blessed by spirit today

♥LjS

228 days of perseverance.
OK then…

I CAN do that, I WILL do that, I AM DOING IT
starting tomorrow.

♥LjS

There is no need for greatness.

The desire 'to be great' diminishes the journey of being.

As the state of being diminishes...therefore does the joy.

Being great brings joy.

To desire greatness brings anything but.

♥LjS

The year of transformation...

Wings are budding

Shells are starting to weaken

Eyes starting to open

Soon freedom from the safe home we once knew
transformation into the vast new world of unlimited
boundaries...

New views as the new way of being in the world
comes into sight.
Keep your balance, focus and always look straight ahead...

All is and will be provided to you.

Transformation equals growth.

You are loved.

We are loved.

Don't be afraid.

♥LjS

As I ponder 2011...

I have come to the conclusion that even though 2011 had its VERY difficult moments, I feel like it's an old friend that came in to teach me many beautiful lessons.

I will be sorry to see it leave.

Thank you 2011, you were a good girlfriend...

Onward and upward

♥LjS

A very wise person told me that everything you have ever put on the Internet stays there forever.

Be careful what you say and do...you never know who's waiting for one wrong move, sad but true. Not to mention how it can be manipulated.

Love and light always... ;)

♥LjS

I think it is so strange to think that one-day when someone...someplace...is researching their genealogy...you and I will be part of it as only a name that lived here or there. We will be the great, great, great grandmother or grandfather to, _____.

What will your legacy be?

♥LjS

If you were given $10,000 to make 'your' life better…

What would you do with it?

♥ LjS

Message of the Moment:

Be fearless...

♥LjS

A mantra for you:

"I refuse to be what anyone wants me to be so THEY feel better about their life. All I can do is be true to me and feel good about mine".

Never be afraid to be who YOU are.

Like minds WILL find you.

The rest will rise up and fall away!

Smile and ALWAYS be proud.

You are loved!

:)

♥LjS

I feel accomplished...

I learned something today about myself.

♥LjS

The need to change everything is overwhelming...just sayin'.

I'm thinking life is too short to NOT change a few things.

Shake the olive tree and see what happens.

I'm tired of the way it is.

I figure its not going to change without me changing it.

So what the hell...

Happy 2012 to me.

Time to take it to the next level.

♥LjS

If we are unwilling to "do our work" it will be done for us!

The universe and our higher selves have a funny way of taking care of what we are afraid to do ourselves.

It's a good thing we have our own backs!

;)

♥LjS

I love Santa.

Remember to be beautiful and shine that light of yours.

Find a moment to bring in peace and gratitude

for what you do have and be the love you seek.

Tonight Santa comes to town.

♥LjS

More light!

Yay! Yipee! Yahoo!

Thank you dark for all you do but the light feels so much better.

Winter solstice....soon it will be spring.

Time to go in and do your work then wake up hungry and ready to take on the world.

I knew I should have been a bear.

♥LjS

Many people like to talk about what they don't have...

Use this time of giving and receiving to share with others what you do have.

xo

♥LjS

So grateful for what I do have...

♥LjS

Am I the only one who feels bad for all the trees that get cut down during Christmas time?????

Maybe they like being outside with the birds in the crisp winter air.

Maybe they don't want to be decorated for our amusement and brought inside to die.

Or

Maybe their purpose is to bring joy and to be of service?

Maybe cutting them down to be used for the holidays is their purpose here on earth?

Guess we could say the same about fresh cut flowers...

Oh life here on earth...

♥LjS

Hmmmm...

In the process of changing everything...

Letting go of everything...and starting all over with everything...

AGAIN

Sometimes I think it is easier then holding on to what isn't working, at least we have a chance that way.

Thinking I'm ok with it...

The struggle of what is, is nothing, compared to the struggle of what can be.

Tom Hanks had it right in the movie Cast Away when he finally left the island.
Wilson?

♥LjS

I think I am way busier when I'm sleeping then when I'm awake.

I can only imagine what tonight will bring.

Still thinking about last night, and the night before that and the night before that...

Nothing is what we think it is.

♥LjS

Take what you are good at...find people who can benefit from what you know and can offer...and change the world!

♥LjS

Nothing is there unless you create it

LjS

We are here to do good in the world...
however we all do that good.

♥LjS

Kids eat what you put in front of them. Give them crap and they will eat it.

Give them things that are good for them and they will eat when hungry enough.

Metaphor…again.

♥LjS

I claim my humanity, therefore my imperfection, although always remaining perfectly imperfect.

We are already perfect just the way we are...

No need to want to be that which we already are.

Got it?

♥LjS

In Detroit we don't have clouds...

We have ONE, GREAT, BIG, GIANT, GRAY blanket
that seems to go on forever and ever. It's only December...
I think I can, I know I can, I think I can, I know I can.

♥LjS

So I am sitting at the restaurant around the corner from my house and I notice this cute young guy sitting next to me.

Slowly all these people started taking pictures with him. Everyone is shaking his hand and asking for his autograph.

When all the people left, I leaned over and said, "I don't mean to be rude but who are you"?

He said, "The quarterback for the Lions",

I said, "Ohhhhhhhh.....ok.....".

Then I leaned over and said to him, "I'm Lisa J. Smith. I'm kind of a big deal in what I do".

He started cracking up.
I said in all seriousness and a straight face, "No, really I am".

Then we both died laughing!

If you can't laugh at yourself, why bother...?

♥LjS

What a day...What a day

♥LjS

Self-deception...

Ahhhh…so fascinating to me.

The only person who truly cares about what we do in the long run is us.

Hence the word 'self'.

How do you SELF DECEIVE YOURSELF?????

Oh life and the human brain...

Kind of like navigating a minefield!!!!

♥LjS

Chuga chuga...

Chuga chuga...

CHOO CHOO

Keep plugging away LIL' BLUE ENGINE

I knew I loved the book,

"The Little Engine that Could".

Next time, I might pick a different favorite book.

The new one will be where the train is already on the downhill.

This is a mighty BIG hill I found myself on!

♥LjS

Sometimes the lives of others and how they choose to live puts perspective on our life. It can help put some things in place. I believe that yet sometimes forget.

MOST everything we concern ourselves with really doesn't matter. What matters most we least concern ourselves with.

Life is over once you blink...100% true. Please do your best to concern yourself with what really matters.

If you don't know what that is...feel your heart.

Do not think with your mind. Life may seem to drag on forever at times...but truly it's a blip.

Be happy and smile...

Be kind and be beautiful...

Smile and know you are love...

Live and love with all your heart while you can...

It really is a gift.

♥LjS

What makes people think they can come to my door...hand
me a pamphlet on their beliefs...
and think what I believe is wrong.

Really???

Hey, I didn't come knocking on your door...

♥LjS

I'm reading an article in Jack Detroit about the massive underground dog-fighting problem in Detroit. What happens to these sweet animals sickens me.

Sometimes I wonder how the good really can overcome all the bad in the world...

I know in my heart we have to keep fighting for animals and for those who have no voice. We have to be strong for those cannot be. We have to be the ones who make a difference.

One person and one act of good at a time can change everything.

We have to...we are needed.

Do good today and please make a difference...

♥LjS

Sometimes far away is not far enough away.

Can you ever be far enough away???

NO, because 'away' is like lint... it just sticks.

Lint roller anyone?

:)

♥LjS

There is a reason why saying, "F*!# it" is so popular...
Just sayin'.

Sometimes that's all there is left to say...

Change what you can and leave the rest.

♥LjS

They say home is where the heart is....

I found my home in Chicago this Thanksgiving week while visiting my daughter.

Thanksgiving is not an easy week for many.   There are many who are separated from their friends and family. Remember there is no time and space.

A home is wherever your heart may take you.

Send your love, open your hearts and know that wherever you are…you are loved. Beam your love to others when not with them…they will feel it.

I'm thinking I'll have to remember that as I leave one "home" for another and head back to the 'D'.

So grateful for all the good I've done in the world

@Alliesmith and @Andrew

♥LjS

As I sit in the bagel shop...

I have seen 3 wonderful acts within a short time.

We will never know how we affect people by the smallest things we do.

I can only wonder what the world would be like if we smiled, loved, helped one another out and said nice things to each other more often.

It may not fix the world...but it just might bring light to the moment.

After all...those moments create the journey.

♥LjS

I am watching Regis on 20/20.

The message to share is we are all have a gift. If we don't follow our gifts…the DREAMS that live in our HEART…

The only people who will be disappointed in us at the end is us.

I have disappointed people, have enemies and a list of people who would love to throw me under the bus with nothing but nasty things to say.

You know what?

They are NOTHING compared to the disappointment that I would have in my heart at the end of my life, for myself, if I did not at least try to follow my heart.

What about you?

Tonight, as I watch Regis leave his show,

I open my heart for the infinite possibilities that lie ahead for all of us if we could only live in our hearts, never stray from our truth, stay authentic and never accept NO for an answer.

♥LjS

Bottom line:

I need to be back on the air...in a studio...doing my thing...

talking to YOU!

I miss my headphones and microphone...darn it!

♥LjS

Maybe ghosts are not called ghosts.

Maybe they don't like being called 'ghosts'.

Maybe they are insulted they are called ghosts.

Maybe what we call ghosts, are the same energies that you and I are now, and that we will be again.

Maybe we are all ghosts now.

"Ghosts" are the same energy you have always been.

Maybe we need to just let it be and stop being so surprised by paranormal activity and call it normal.

Maybe we need to start asking different questions.

Maybe we need to start learning and educating each other about what these energies are…not what they can do.

When after all they are just you and I.

♥LjS

I found some old shows from June 2010.

I'm feeling a little sad missing all of you yet knowing my time spent now, not working on the air, was much needed.

I am looking forward to a time when we all meet again.

What a ride...what a ride.

♥LjS

ENERGY...

If we only knew what we were all capable of…
I'm always learning this again and again.

It's funny it is not easy to be what we are naturally.

Years of living in our humanity, even lifetimes of living,
have made us defensive, hard, tense and unnatural in our
being and movement.

I have said for years,
"change your perspective...change you life".
I'm not sure that we can even begin to imagine the
unlimited possibilities we have within us.

We will know when we begin to train our perspectives
therefore our minds to focus back on what IS...

back to Ki....

Practicing what we ALREADY made of in the first place…

Fascinating

♥LjS

You really do have all the answers.

Don't be afraid to trust that you, alone, are enough!

♥LjS

Ok, it's like this…
We have good days, bad days and all days in between.

Some days we are served a WHOLE BUNCH of stuff we
LOVE, others days not so much.

Everything is always MOVING, nothing stays the same…

If you believe that it is the same…you are FOOLING
yourself into a false state of stagnation and then 'it' becomes
thicker.

Be free…
Move…

Let things come up and out and loosen up little…good or
bad…it's all a moment.

That is about the only thing you can count on.
Don't try to guess where the wind is coming from and
THEN want to go with it…you will have nothing left.

Stay loose and free…

Let the wind come and dance around you. FEEL it…then
when it blows through you and it's gone say, "thank you"
and let it be.

Oh yea…

Have each other's backs will ya???

♥LjS

NEW DAY...NEW DAY...

Do I hear a Greek salad calling my name???

Don't forget to put your shoulders back and be the 'ROCK STARS' you were born to be.

Hey, even if it only lasts for a few minutes it's better than no minutes at all!

♥LjS

Homework for the day:

Be the 'love' today that other people are seeking...

♥LjS

Aren't we all just saying the same thing...

♥LjS

New tattoo idea for my wrist:

O. M. A. A. T.
One Moment At A Time

Sorry mom, I just need the daily reminder.

♥ LjS

I am a manifesting fool...just sayin' :)

♥LjS

New day...

♥LjS

Is it already a full moon again???

I just looked outside...

My goodness it is beautiful tonight!

I think I'm glad it's getting darker sooner...

more time to enjoy the light of the dark night sky.

Awww, the sweet release of what no longer serves us
anymore...

only to bring in the cycle of all that is new.

OK, off to admire the greatness!

♥LjS

Let's not make things more complicated than they are,
especially when it comes to energy and the "spirit world".

It's not that complex.
It's just misunderstood.

It's just re-learning to look at these things differently.

♥LjS

People always say that "every one is replaceable".

I'm thinking that just isn't so!

Be who you are…not who others want you to be.

If someone thinks you're replaceable, they have their head in the wrong place…

Consider yourself blessed, say thank you and MOVE ON!

The universe is looking out for YOU.

YOU know who you are!

♥LjS

Watching my cats play brings me such joy.

They are an education about people and life.

The strategies they use in 'play'
are a great metaphor for life...

Patience

Fun

Hide and Seek

Look before you leap

Don't take anything personal

Good stuff!

♥LjS

Back in the motor city... for now.

I'm ready to go again.

Leaving my suitcase out.

♥LjS

The healing we seek happens on so many levels.

Instead of trying to figure it all out, just allow it to be.

The healing is happening anyway.

We may as well believe.

♥LjS

....As the old shifts and breaks away, the new comes in and continues to keep the wheels in motion.

Always evolving and propelling us into the great unknown...

All just a cycle

All just a moment

All the beauty of all that is

Off to do my thing...

Whatever that may be today...

Full of promise and opportunities to do our best...

Just for today.

♥LjS

Sitting in the airport...

My thought is there are so many people who have no job and then we wonder why?

Everything is automated and no human is needed for the conveniences we have come to expect and can't live without.

We complain we have no jobs and the economy is horrible yet we want what we want.

The industrial revolution did the same thing... and we built upon that.

Maybe the work is being done behind the scenes and we just can't see it?

♥LjS

New…

New day...

New month...

New moment...

New energy.

:)

♥LjS

No matter how we cross over and 'change form', we are always ALL ok on the 'other side'.

We are always loved on this side.

We are forever connected on all sides.

♥LjS

Message of the Moment:

Keep your nose to the grindstone and keep going...

♥LjS

It always feels so good to get rid of the yuck and clean out
what we don't need anymore.

We never see the filth when we are in it.

Only after it is clean, do we see how dirty it really was,
PERSPECTIVE!!!!

The energy of what we don't need anymore feels heavy and
wears us down…sometimes it even makes us tired and sick.

If we don't clean our house, it will be cleaned for us.

Boy do I know that!!!

What I also know:

It's all in the highest and best and boy does it feel GOOD to
be clean, however our "stuff" gets cleaned!

Sometimes the scrubbing irritates us…but boy it's worth it!

I love 'cleaning house' and grateful that that it was cleaned
for me when I did not have the energy to clean it myself…

See we really are loved!

♥LjS

Pet Peeve:

Butt kissers, especially when it is so obvious…

EWWWW

♥LjS

Word of the day:

Germinating

:)

♥LjS

Germinating: present participle of ger·mi·nate (Verb)
Verb: (of a seed or spore) Begin to grow and put out shoots
after a period of dormancy.

♥ LjS

I have learned that there is no talking 'with' or 'to' spirit, there is only "being with".
From that...comes all 'communication'.

The 'talking to' soothes the monkey mind...the 'being with' soothes the soul.

♥LjS

Scripts within Scripts within Scripts within Scripts...

All so interesting.

♥LjS

Funny how people hear what they want...

♥LjS

Hindsight is 20/20...

The key is to not beat yourself up for not seeing what was right in front of you all along.

Maybe you were not supposed to see?

Maybe you were looking but didn't want to see?

Either way, the key is letting those days be in the past to create newer, bigger and better things for today.

Move on from what was and into what is.

♥LjS

...Or maybe everything is just as it needs to be

;)

♥LjS

I think something is missing.

♥LjS

Watching TV is like being a witness of an illusionary world.

It is very much like the Spirit world watching us.
They view us living our lives on the "TV" of life here on
Earth.

When you watch TV it is easy to yell at the TV, see the
outcome, direct the characters, see what is best for the
characters, etc.

Start to look at your life as a viewer (witness) and see
everything as a "story".

Maybe life will not get the best of you...you will get the best
of life!

♥LjS

Wisdom has a funny way of showing up...

I'm thinking that it's not always what you read in books, even though many experts of self-help want you to think it is...

Wisdom is far to wise for that.

♥LjS

True divinity allows for error

LjS

To be imperfectly imperfect…

Ahhhh to BE

♥LjS

My vision statement:

To help people realize what they already know. "Mission statements change but vision statements never do".

Thank you @alliejsmith

You are wise beyond your years.

♥LjS

I have been thinking about how to explain
to people what I do.

I came up with this, "I help people see things differently".

When asked 'how' I say,

"By telling them what they already know".

When they ask me to prove it I say,

"That is not my job".
Mine is to serve…and tell you what I get.

My first obligation is to spirit, to tell you what they are
saying, then to myself and then to you!

Take it or leave it.

Again, the choice is always yours!!!

♥LjS

Maybe baseball fields are so green because the players spit on them so much…it keeps the field moist and lush.

Just sayin'

♥LjS

I went to a nursing home today.

I realized how grateful I am for what I have TODAY.

Again, humbled into seeing how important this moment is
right now and appreciating what I do have.

You never really know what you have until
you see what can be.

Gratitude for what we have because we never know what
life will serve up.

No one is better than anyone else.
You are not defined by what you have...

♥LjS

Thought of the Moment:

Do and be the things you will be proud of when you look back on your life...

There are many things I would love to post, say and complain about.

I know that they will not make me proud of who I am.

In the mean time, I will be as my late Grandma Jessie and my mom taught me,

To always put on a smile, put my shoulders back, be the better person and keep my chin up.

I do that so that one day I can be someone my kids can be proud of.

:)

♥LjS

Sometimes...
People are only as good as the butt they are kissing.
They do that to save their own...

Just sayin'

♥LjS

"Yes" needs to become the new "no".

♥LjS

OK my turn…

please

♥ LjS

An entire day to do whatever I want...

I don't know what to do!

♥LjS

Hard work is hard work...

You can't define it or judge the work that is being done.

Just ask the Karate Kid!

♥LjS

IMAGINE YOUR 80TH BIRTHDAY…

WHO WILL BE THERE WITH YOU?

WHAT TRIBUTE WOULD YOU LIKE THEM TO
MAKE ABOUT YOUR LIFE?

FOR ME IT IS:

That I reached my goals and that my perseverance through
rough times inspired others to reach their goals. That
through it all I made the world better with my positive and
life changing contributions. That I loved my family with all
my being, always believed that anything was possible and I
always did my best.

NOW TELL ME YOURS…

♥ LjS

I'm thinking this is about the time I R E A L L Y start to miss summer time. Rain, cold, windy, dreary, leaves falling turning soon to cold wet YUCK!!!

Wake me up in April...

WAIT!!!

DOES THAT MEAN I AM NOT LIVING IN THE MOMENT????

:)

♥LjS

Personalities...
Personalities sell products.

♥ LjS

I wish I thought of Starbucks first.

Explaining coffee is so much easier...

♥LjS

I heard through the grapevine today that there are an awful lot of people who need a little pick me up and are feeling a little blue.

I can't reach you all right now the way I did before.   In the meantime my message to you is:

Hang in there...you will be ok!

This is just a moment.

You are shedding old stuff and sometimes it hurts.

The beauty is what lies underneath...keep going!

When we open the door to "spirituality" as we call it,

know that we are seeing things from a new and different perspective that we have not seen from before.

THAT is why it rocks our boat!

I think it is time for a little of our

SPIRITUAL ROCK STAR WARRIOR KICK ASS

time together...

Stay Tuned

I'm thinking of you too!

♥LjS

"The Help", yes I cried my eyes out.

So much to think about and so many layers!

As much as people are not good and treat each other badly, there are always the FEW good ones who make me feel proud!

The funny thing is, one good person brings more good to the world than all the crappy people that bring bad.

In the long run, as I used to tell my kids when they were little, "the good guy always wins...even if it does not seem like it at times".

Authenticity is so beautiful!!!

I know and whole lot of "crappy" people who fool us into believing they are the 'good ones.'

It would shock you to know who they are.

The funny thing is in the scheme of things they are so UNIMPORTANT.

WHY?

The good of the heart will always win.

Amazing how with one drop of kindness, you can change one person's life!

♥LjS

I just received another "SIGN" that the universe does us favors in the strangest of ways.

We may NOT like them, but man...I am CONVINCED someone, somewhere is looking out for us.

Now, if only karma would catch up with.....

Oh it will! ;)

No need to concern ourselves with other peoples stuff...ours is more than enough.

Wishing karma is creating karma...

Smile and stay in your own cup and say thank you!!!!

♥LjS

Remember to pay it forward and be kind to someone today.

Give them a chance to let them show you their heart.

You never know what dominoes you are setting off.

Remember, everything comes full circle!

♥LjS

My peeps are saying to me…
"Say nothing right now".
I'm thinking that might be a good idea because nothing good is going to come out if I open up my mouth!

♥LjS

The root of all that we seek most of the time is
VALIDATION and ACCEPTANCE
not love...
LOVE does not seek approval, it simply just is.
The 'whys' are our journeys.
PLEASE be accepting of WHO YOU ARE.
It's OK if no one else accepts that, I PROMISE.
Just learn to validate and accept YOU...
That is LOVE

♥LjS

I'm wearing all black today.

I am in mourning.

I already miss you summer time.

Until the next time we meet again,

I'll try to keep my spirits up and my head held high until

spring comes back.

You live forever in my heart...

No joke!

♥LjS

I am so happy to report for all those who do not understand our proposals, our ideologies, our business plans, our ideas, our visions, our possibilities, our intent, our talents or what WE CAN BRING TO THE TABLE...

(due to the many hours stuck in a box, having narrow visions, being afraid to take a leap and build something new)

Our message to you is:

THANK YOU!!

You are making our load much less to carry by helping us weed our gardens.

WE NOW KNOW what will NOT work for US either.

WE can now focus on what will...

Business is business and maybe YOUR needs don't meet OURS!!!

From all of us...who are NOT afraid to create change and willing to risk it all for what we know is possible...

See you in the boardroom...

and this time we will be the decision makers!

♥LjS

I am telling you this NOT for a, "Oh wow that was so nice", "Oh good for you" or "That was really awesome of you Lisa". I AM telling you this so that you will be inspired to perform a random act of kindness.

There is always SOMETHING we can do for someone to help them have a smiley day.

I was in the drive thru, and as I sometimes do, I paid for the person behind me. By the way, with no job I was thinking to myself, "What are you doing Lisa???"
(It just felt like the right thing to do in the moment).

I remembered what I always say to my clients and listeners, "We need not have excuses on why we cant, we must only be in the action of why we can". The girl in the window did not know what to say. She looked back at me with a blank stare.

She said, "But they ordered 2 things"!

I said, "Ok...well I am paying for whatever they ordered". She was flustered and didn't know what to do. She had to ask her manager first.

Before leaving I said, "Please tell him I said to have a nice day". She was so unnerved by this offering it was actually kind of funny. Maybe the lesson was for her too!

As I always say, "Nothing is EVER what we think or why we think it is. We just have to listen to the inner voice that guides and then act. If you feel guided to do something for someone...it might just change their life or maybe even yours"! I feel accomplished and it only took a split second decision and a few dollars...I'm not worried about the money.
I know that I am blessed and will always be provided for.

♥LjS

Beauty is wasted on the youth...

the older I get the more I get this.

♥LjS

Where there is smoke there is fire…it's common sense.

Funny how we always forget that, huh?

♥LjS

Give people what they THINK they want and they will flock to you.

Give people something they have never seen before and they flee.

Why?

Because people fear what they do not know.

Knowing what we don't know might just set us free.

It just might be worth walking into unknown territory to find out.

Funny someone else did that...and made people work for it.

He NEVER gave them what they wanted...

only the tools that they needed for success.

MANY did not follow...

Now MANY worship him...

We don't practice what we preach...

♥LjS

I have come to the conclusion that people make things harder than they need to be.

The truth is, if they just did their job rather making things more complicated, they just might get something done.

Spend less time trying to look like you know what your doing and DO IT...

♥LjS

You know, the more I think of it, the more I like just about anything more than PEOPLE at times.

PEOPLE, I'm beginning to think, are as crazy as they are good. No wonder the world is what it is.

We all point fingers at Washington, at each other, we throw each other under the bus, we fight in wars and we don't know what we are fighting about, we blame everything on the economy, we blame the President, regardless of the party and the list goes on.

ENOUGH ALREADY!

YOU ARE THE ECONOMY AND YOU ARE WASHINGTON.

Maybe it's time to start looking in the mirror if YOU WANT THINGS TO CHANGE!

OK…better now!

♥LjS

I love those stories of children connecting with "invisible friends".

It reminds me of how at one time, before no one told us no, we believed in all that is!

♥LjS

We cannot teach what we have not lived.

To teach that what we have learned is to share life.

To teach we must experience living.

♥LjS

The question:

"How do you deal with a person who is

(_____ fill in the blank)" ?

The answer:

You don't have to 'deal' with them once you understand who they really are...

As I say, "information is knowledge and knowledge is wisdom".

Wisdom says it's not worth it.

;)

♥LjS

Message of the Moment:

Always trust your intuition and follow your hunches even if it doesn't make sense at the time.

If there are red flags, there is a reason they are there.

If people don't seem authentic, then they probably aren't.

If you feel a load of crap is being shoveled your way,

know its crap and will smell worse the closer it gets to you.

Don't accept it.

If you are uncomfortable…leave.

We really are amazing if we would just believe in ourselves and trust we will be OK!

♥LjS

Message of the Moment:

What goes around comes around...

100%

♥ LjS

Message of the Moment:

LOVE today on 9/11.

Remember those who you love and those who made a difference in your life.

Love everyday!

♥LjS

Message of the Moment:

Don't be afraid to be who you are.

Shine YOUR LIGHT bright…as bright as you can.

We will find you.

We will find each other.

You DO know who you are.

You do know it is ok to feel what you feel.

You know stuff.

Trust what you know.

Life is good…smile and know you are loved.

Until next time…remember wherever in the world you are I am too!

♥LjS

TAKING MY POWER BACK...

;)

♥LjS

Message of the Moment:

HEY "ROCK STARS"

(and there can only be one)

Do me a favor and go look in your mirror.

When you see a person looking back at you say,

"Hey, hey, hey, ROCK STAR, what do you say"?

By the way...

That thing about there only being only "one" rock star, it's true.

It's YOU!

How else do you think you made it this far???

♥LjS

Message of the Moment:

No one ever said it was easy.

♥LjS

Message of the Moment:

Nothing that anyone EVER does is about you personally.
Sometimes we just stand in the line of fire.

As much as it might hurt, we have to pull ourselves up and
out of the situation.

Look with different eyes at the situation
and you will see the truth!

♥ LjS

Message of the Moment:

We are here to be human…we already are spiritual.

I say it all the time!!!

If we work more on honoring our humanity and not always worry about the spiritual....

(a.k.a. being more grounded and earthly)

maybe we would "lighten up" a little.

Just so you know, being gentle and HONEST with yourself as a human being is the key to that which you seek spiritually.

♥LjS

Message of the Moment:

Sometimes you just have to stop worrying about it.

♥LjS

Message of the Moment:

If there are truly 1000's of different parts of me being played out in any given moment, in parallel worlds, I figure that is more than I can control.

Thousands of lives? I can hardly take care of one. One is more than enough for me to manage right now.

I'll just let go and let all the other parts of me take care of all my needs.

All because just 'me' can do no such thing!

♥LjS

Message of the Moment:

Your path is where you choose to walk.

♥LjS

Message of the Moment:

Grow where you are planted.

I like it.

♥LjS

Before honor comes humility

♥LjS

Don't cry for what you have lost…
rejoice for all that you have gained

♥LjS

Be the piece of peace

LjS

It's hard to hate what got me here.

♥LjS

Message of the Moment:

Sometimes we have to follow the trail backwards to go back to the beginning.

The problem is we can't always find the trail.

I suppose that is when we start a new one.

♥LjS

Message of the Moment:

When trying to hold on to water you just end up all wet.

♥LjS

Message of the Moment:

_____

YOU fill in the blank!

♥LjS

Message of the Moment:

There is NO PLAN B

♥ LjS

Message of the Moment:

By the time you finish reading this...the moment is gone and
you are on to a new one...

So can we ever really be in 'the' moment
we THINK we are???

It depends on what moment you are talking about...you see
there are millions of moments in every single moment...

So what is your moment?

♥LjS

Life is too short.

I am beginning to see spending it in a way that is less than you desire, less than you have dreamed of, or less than you deserve, is certainly not worth anything at all in the big picture of all that is.

The value comes in the living and experiencing of your dreams. They would not come to you if they were not meant to be lived.

Life is not for wanting, lacking and living in unhappiness.

Your choice always.

Live as you want because in the end it's your story...

Choose wisely.

♥LjS

It is within the letting go...the pieces come together. When you let go with your heart of one thing, the healing begins. The heart then begins to feel love in a deeper way.

Many wonderful things will come when releasing.

Hanging on is an illusion.

The letting go is the reality and door opener.

Faith baby.

Who has it?????

The brave and the strong.

♥LjS

Big picture vs. Little picture...

Which way do you intend to view your experiences and life?

Nothing is as it appears.

Nothing is what you think.

Where are you directing your thoughts?

Creation comes from perspective.

What is your perspective of the situations in your life?

Take a look, do inventory and

"Change your perspective to change your life".

;)

♥LjS

Message of the Moment:

If you make yourself OVERLY important...

Then you really are NOT as important as you think...

Just sayin'

♥LjS

As the night falls upon the day do you ever stop to think that today was one less day that you had to make a difference?

It's one less day to enjoy life?

It's one less day to enjoy the little things?

One less day to live as YOU?

Tonight look back on your day.

Was it beautiful?

Can you find the beauty even in the chaos?

It's one less day you have to be all that you can be.

Better get to work...

Time waits for no one.

♥LjS

Message of the Moment:

There is much strength in defeat and surrender.

Holding on and fighting brings much weakness.

Letting go brings relief.

♥LjS

Message of the Moment:

For today:

Expect nothing, be surprised by nothing and allow life to be what it is...just life!

You are you and others are others.

What you do is because that is what you do.

What they do is because that is what they do.

It's all part of a role we are playing. One day, in some other lifetime, you may not be the giver that you are today!

You just might be like them.

So let it be and set your heart free.

♥LjS

Message of the Moment:

Pssssst

Spread the word…

We are not special because of what we can or cannot do.

We are special because we simply just are WHO WE ARE!

Ahhh, the illusions to create separations all to keep us in our place…

Step over them and through them.

You will see the only differences are the ones that we create.

♥LjS

Message of the Moment:

Imagine there are two hoses connected to your stomach.

As pain is being sucked out, it is being replaced with love.

Use the disappointments and hurts from others to change

your pain into strength.

As the love passes through the hose and into YOU,

know you are now being filled with love.

Alchemy...it is all one love.

You can change anything from one thing to another.

TRY IT!

♥LjS

Message of the Moment:

Failure is a part of success...

If you cannot handle the failures

then you are NOT ready for the success.

You can quote me on that!

♥LjS

Message of the Moment:

Thank God it is all just a moment!

;)

♥LjS

Message of the Moment:

I was quoted today so thought I would share:

"Just by being born, you have already changed the world".
Lisa J. Smith (2011)

♥LjS

I'm pretty sure I am just about over the cosmic jokes

right about now...

Wake me up when they are over!

You????

♥LjS

Message of the Moment:

Trust your gut

Never sell out

Be who you are

Speak your truth

Don't do what you do for money or fame.

Be willing to close one door so that the next one will open.

If someone does not like you just walk on and do your thing.

(There will always be someone who doesn't and that's ok)

Hold your head high and be the ROCK STAR you were born to be!

You CAN never go wrong!

♥LjS

Message of the Moment:

Reiki Rocks

♥LjS

Message of the Moment:

Who are you????

WHO? WHO? WHO?

The answer just might surprise if you if you give it a little
thought!

♥LjS

Message of the Moment:

What do you REALLY believe?

Think about it…what you thought you believed might not
be what you believed at all?

♥LjS

Message of the Moment:

What you put in…is what you put out!

Work, food, relationships, effort, etc.

Become AWARE!

♥LjS

Message of the Moment:

YOU CAN DO IT.

Even when you think you can't...

you can

you do

and you will.

You have ALREADY proven that.

;)

♥LjS

Message of the Moment:

THANK YOU for being YOU.

I thank ME for being ME.

Things are divinely perfect.

Remember to give thanks for what you DO have.

What you don't 'think' you have, really doesn't matter,

since it really doesn't exist anyway, right?

It's ALL-good!

"IRIE" as my Rasta & Jamaican friends say!

♥LjS

Message of the Moment:

Thank you for the strength I ALREADY have.

Thank you for the STRENGTH I already have.

THANK YOU for the strength I already have.

Say it out loud as many times as you can...

Give thanks for what you ALREADY do have,

Let that gratitude manifest into

all that you dream!

♥LjS

Message of the Moment:

Be the leader of change...

end of story!

♥LjS

Message of the Moment:

L I V E

♥ LjS

Maybe we are all a little "Para" normal

♥ LjS

Message of the Moment:

Sometimes the only way to see what you do have, is to see what you do not have.

Look back to see how far you have come.

Look forward in order to stay open to what is coming

♥LjS

Message of the Moment:

I really have no message except for this:

I wish for each and every one of you to be the best you can be in this moment.

Let all the other moments be what they are and let this one be what it is.

♥LjS

Message of the Moment:

Ok...

We may not understand why things are the way they are.

I'm thinking maybe we don't need to understand the why.

♥LjS

Message of the Moment:

Those who say they 'are', aren't.

Those who say they 'aren't', are.

This has been proven time and time again.

♥LjS

Message of the Moment:

Trust what you KNOW!

You KNOW it for a reason.

Are you listening to it?

♥LjS

Message of the Moment:

Everything is only a moment

Ok carry on…

♥LjS

…. And if all else fails

and you've tried everything

and none of it seemed to work...

Send love to animals, people, situations, arguments, falling outs, wars, misunderstandings, politicians, oil spills, CEOS, countries, friends, not so good of friends, co workers, bosses, cities, etc.

Hey, if nothing else seems to be working…

what do you have to lose, right????

Try it and let me know how you feel. They will feel better and so will you.

At least you gave it a chance.

♥LjS

If you can't change one thought...

Replace it with another you can't let go of.

At least you changed it, right?

Maybe with something good?

Just a new thought...

♥LjS

Expectations can only lead to disappointments.

Expect nothing from no one

and you will never be let down.

Sounds cynical, right???

It's not.

If you are living in your moment for YOU and you are doing your thing and expecting nothing…

anyone and anything that happens is the only icing on YOUR cake.

Create you...

♥LjS

I'm thinking that's all I have for NOW.

I'm pretty sure my life will give me more inspiration tomorrow.

Actually, I can pretty much guarantee it.

I do have this…

Thank you 'teachers' from long ago...

for making me who I am today.

I always dreamed of today.

♥LjS

If you KNOW your value

If you KNOW who you are

and if you really are OK with who you are...

I'm thinking that what others think, say, do, or do not do...

does not really matter.

Do what you do...

and as someone said to me not so long ago....

"Let all stuff that does not belong to you

roll off like water off a ducks back".

Think about it…that makes sense!

♥LjS

Those people who said they loved you, who said you were so special and then can leave so easily...send them love.

The love is for you not them.

♥LjS

Gratitude for what you do have will lead to gratitude for what you will have.

♥LjS

Message of the Moment:

Some people are like fleas.

They jump on anything alive and moving.

They feed off life.

Don't forget your flea collar when you go out.

You never know where the lil' buggers are hiding.

I think I said this before, but it deserves repeating.

♥LjS

Message of the Moment:

If you KNOW your value you will know who you are.

Then you really are OK with who you are...

♥LjS

So my new thought for the moment:

If you have nothing nice to say....don't say anything at all.

If you are truly who you say you are, and
you say you are from love and light, then be it.

Stop talking about it.

ACTIONS SPEAK LOUDER THAN WORDS.

♥LjS

The end....the middle....the beginning.

♥LjS

Some of those who say they are act as if they are anything but what they say they are...

They say they 'are' because they need to believe they fit in SOMEWHERE.

Send them love so they do!

♥LjS

Funny when someone says that you are projecting...

aren't they projecting?

♥LjS

Why are they not sending love instead of words full of daggers?

♥LjS

Friends come and go...

Maybe they were never friends?

Maybe they were just people that you once knew?

Maybe they were just people you crossed paths with?

Some good and some not so good...

Either way you remain you.

You always have you.

♥LjS

The ones you send love to might never know they got it.

It's not for them to get…it's for you to heal.

Love yourself enough to let go and not go there ever again.

♥LjS

WOW, the people you once loved can hurt you so BAD.

At times it hurts so much so it rips your heart out and leaves a tear in your soul.

It feels like your heart is going to break open...

We can only send love.

It just feels better.

♥LjS

You don't have to say "I forgive you". You just need to find it in your heart and let it go.

Forgiving is for you...

What is for you ends up being for all anyway.

How can it not be?

♥LjS

Wondering how many times you have to forgive...

I suppose as many times as it takes.

♥LjS

.

Nothing like doing some down right earthly stuff to ground yourself!

Love it.

♥LjS

ONE:

Owning Now Eternally

♥LjS

Winning is the illusion.

There is nothing to 'win' when you've already won.

WIN:

Wanting Invisible Nothingness

vs.

WON:

Wonderment Of Now

♥LjS

Just sayin'…

One day all will be good in the world again.

Nothing and no one is what you think.

One day we will remember that and
ALL WILL BE LOVE

AGAIN!

:)

♥LjS

Can I be done being humbled?

Just sayin'

♥LjS

Message of the Moment:

"Now I lay me down to sleep, I pray tonight the answers seep. For when they seep, as I am sure they will, tomorrows day will fill thy will".

Who says I can't write poetry?!?!

Sweet dreams

:)

♥LjS

Message of the Moment:

Only believe what you know to be true within yourself.

How others perceive you and what they may like or dislike about you really does not matter!

What ONLY matters is how you perceive yourself.

Maybe that is what needs to change...

Now go change 'the world' today!

♥LjS

Message of the Moment:

BE YOUR OWN ROCK STAR!

If you are not going to be that for yourself...

NO ONE ELSE IS EITHER!

Sorry not my rules...

I have to live with them too!

♥LjS

People are just people.

We often see their true character when backed into a corner.
Sometimes that true character was there along.

Usually we refuse to believe it because we see what we want
because we are afraid the truth will be more than we can
handle.

You never get more than you can handle.

Open your eyes…trust and have faith…you can do this.

And move on…

♥LjS

If it's true that all dogs have their day…and cats have really do have nine lives, wouldn't you rather be a dog?

At least it's only a day.

♥LjS

Speaking our truth can get us into trouble.
The more I realize this, the more I want to speak my truth.
Not to get in trouble…
but so then I know where we all stand.

The truth will set you free.

♥LjS

We never say goodbye...we only say until next time!

♥LjS

Lisa J. Smith's Cup Theory

There are seven billion cups on the planet. Each one of us represent one of those cups. The cups symbolizes our physical bodies. What's inside the cup symbolizes the essence of who we are. We are all from the same place, we are just having different experiences in different cups around the world.

We are responsible for our own cup and what goes in it. The problem is, we are so busy in everyone else's cup, we are too busy to manage what is going on in our own cup. If you are in someone else's cup, then anyone can jump into yours.

We are each here having individual experiences in our own cups. The cups give us boundaries, structure, individuality and independence. They keep us safe and protected. The liquid represents us, as an individual, yet all coming from the same source.

Day after day I teach people about, "staying in their own cup". Daily I have to remind myself of the same thing. I am all for helping others, supporting and lending a hand. I truly believe life is a team effort. I also believe we 'think' it is our job to care for others before caring for ourselves. That is backwards thinking. We are here to take care of ourselves first. By "staying in our own cup", we then have the energy and life force to authentically give to others.

Our kids will be ok. Our spouses are fine. Our families will all be taken care. Our bills will be paid. Our co-workers will be fine without us in their business.

My questions to you are these: Why do we always have to jump cups? Why can't we all just stay in our own cup? Why is it that your cup is so unimportant and other people's cups are more appealing than your own?

We are all here to learn, evolve and grow. We are here to remember to respect others and allow them their space to grow, learn and evolve as well. By respecting others, we are respecting ourselves.

Stay in your own cup. Have your own experiences. Don't let other people in your cup. In other words, keep your boundaries and respect others by allowing them their boundaries as well.

We are so busy jumping cups that we don't ever take the time to learn about what is in our cup. This is how we lose our identity, sense of empowerment and therefore ourselves.

It is time to take a swim around my cup and see how it's holding up. I encourage you to do the same!

Much love,

Lisa J. Smith

Afterward

Reflecting back over the past 36 months has been quite an experience. An experience I never thought I would find myself in. Ups, downs, good days, bad days, lessons, letting go, forgiving, finding gratitude in the smallest of details and motivation in whatever I could.

I learned that as far as I have come I am only in the middle of my journey. I am still learning about who I am, what I do and about the dreams I have. I am finding my voice and remembering my strength, wisdom and courage.

As I edited and re-edited 36 Months, I re-read each and every entry a dozen times at least. The memories came crashing back of almost every post. Where I was, how I felt and what inspired each thought. I vacillated back and forth as to whether to write a brief description of where I was and what I was referring to when I wrote them. After much consideration, I decided that I wanted you to feel the way you feel about each post, not the way I felt. Each post not only has deep meaning for me but also for the people who have read them from my social media pages.

I have always loved hearing different peoples interpretations of the same piece of art. I believe language and experiences are based upon each person's own paradigms and experiences. Those experiences define our view of the world. There have been times that people have disagreed with what was written and that is ok. As I look back, I realize I was not seeking approval I was only seeking a place to heal.

I believe that sometimes you have to go backwards to see how far you have come. As I sit and read over what is now become part of my history, I sit in amazement of how much the human spirit can withstand. I learned that when we open ourselves up to receive, what comes out for the most part are positive thoughts and love…over and over and over again.

My wish for you is that you find motivation, empowerment, smiles, wisdom and joy as you read 36 Months. I encourage you to track your journey as well. Your experiences as you move through your life are your story. We all have a story. Sometimes stepping back and looking at your story will show you your own perseverance. Your posts, thoughts, ponderings, reflections and experiences serve as your history. Expressing yourself and speaking your truth becomes liberating. Finding your voice is healing.

If I have learned anything from the work that I do as an intuitive, it's that life moves quickly. We have only one shot to live in every moment. In the end, it is only ourselves we have to answer too. I have also learned from my experiences as an earthly being that we can become caught in our own emotional web and fall victim to others criticisms and beliefs about who they think we are. It's only when we can re-read our own history, do we sometimes see who we really are and not what other people believe.

I have included extra pages for you to track your journey. I hope that you also go back and use the blank spaces on each page to write down your own pearls of wisdom to reflect upon. You will be amazed at how far you have come, too.

Remember that life is a journey and full of experiences. I have learned that there is no good and bad there simply just

..n we can get out of our own way and allow ..xperiences to move through us, we can move through the rough patches much faster.

Life is up to you. How you react and view the world is up to you. I, like everything in my life, am learning that the hard way. It is never too late to find your voice, learn to love yourself and laugh in the face of life. It's not that life won't get to you at times, because it will. You become how you choose to react to it. It's your reaction that will either set you free or keep you in the place you were in.

Use the following pages to write, draw and express yourself. Remember your actions become your history. What do you want your history to look like?

Lisa J. Smith

NOTES

NOTES

NOTES

About the Author

Lisa J. Smith is a mother, daughter, sister, granddaughter and friend. There is nothing she loves more than spending time with her children, Allie and Andrew, her cats Lola and Ming and "her best girlfriend ever", Steve. She was born in Detroit, MI and continues to make her home in the suburbs of Detroit.

Lisa is an intuitive that works one on one with her clients, makes appearances at business conferences, women's groups and paranormal events. She guides and teaches people on how to work with their own intuition as well as motivation and empowerment.

Lisa J. Smith has also worked in the media. She lectures on several topics from self-improvement and empowerment to the development and education of what intuition is and is not.

Her dream is to travel the globe inspiring and uplifting people of all demographics to live in their fullest potential.

You can find Lisa J. Smith on her web site:
www.lisajsmith.com

We hoped you enjoyed this Peeps Publishing book.

Please visit:

<u>www.peepspublishing.com</u>

Continue to follow Lisa J. Smith on her social media pages:

 Facebook.com/lisajsmithfans

 Twitter.com/lisajsmith

Peeps Publishing

PP

Made in the USA
Lexington, KY
07 March 2012